LLANTEG: A PI

A second

Titles published by Llanteg Local History Society

Llanteg Down The Years (2000)
Llanteg: The Days Before Yesterday (2001)
Llanteg House Histories to 1900 (2001) - locally produced booklet
Llanteg: Turning Back The Clock (2002)
Grave and Memorial Inscriptions in Crunwere Parish (2002) -
                                     locally produced booklet
A Brief History of Llanteg Women's Institute 1948-2000 (2003) -
                                     locally produced booklet
Histories of Older Houses in the Parish of Crunwere 1901-2001
                        (2004) - locally produced booklet
Llanteg: A Century In Photographs 1850s to 1950s (2004)
Llanteg: A Picture Book Of Memories 1850s to 1950s (2005)
Llanteg Village Recipe Book (2005) - locally produced booklet

Supported by
The National Lottery
Awards for all Wales scheme

LLANTEG
A PICTURE BOOK
OF MEMORIES
1850s to 1950s

A second memento of our village families

Compiled by:
Ruth Roberts
Edited by:
Judith Lloyd

LLANTEG LOCAL HISTORY SOCIETY
Sandy-Grove, Llanteg, Narberth, Pembrokeshire, SA67 8QG, U.K.

LLANTEG: A PICTURE BOOK OF MEMORIES 1850s TO 1950s

First published in Great Britain 2005 by
LLANTEG LOCAL HISTORY SOCIETY
Sandy-Grove, Llanteg, Narberth, Pembrokeshire, SA67 8QG, U.K.

British Library Cataloguing-in-Publication Data.
A catalogue record for this book is available
from the British Library.

ISBN: 0-9538142-4-6

Front cover photograph - Bessie Morris of Furzy Park with her sister Maggie, seated.
Back cover photograph - Leslie Phillips, 'Lel', of Middleton with Bertie James of Broomylake.

Prepared for printing by *Manuscript ReSearch* (Book Producers)
PO Box 33, Bicester, Oxon, OX26 4ZZ, U.K.
Tel: 01869 323447/322552
Printed and bound by Hackman Printers, Tonypandy, Rhondda.

ACKNOWLEDGEMENTS

*'It is said that every human being dies twice –
once when his body dies and finally when he is actually
forgotten.'*

One of our main aims as a History Society is to make sure that all the inhabitants of Crunwere and Llanteg are remembered for as long as possible.

Little did I expect when I was putting together our first Picture Book in 2003/04 that I would be helping to compile a second Picture Book so soon. It quickly became clear that we had far more photographs than could be accommodated in the first volume. It was a very difficult task to have to sort out which to use and which to leave out - we wanted to include them all! It was because of this that we decided to go ahead immediately and compile this second volume, again featuring pictures up to the 1950s. We thought it would be much easier while we still had photographs on loan, rather than returning them and then trying to collect them all again at a later date. So the History Society would like to repeat its thanks to those who lent us photographs and who have been so understanding and patient while we held on to them.

In the first Picture Book we tried to have some photographs from each old Llanteg family for the period prior to the 1950s, but obviously, as some families were very hard to obtain pictures for, you will find that not all of these families are represented here. However we have done our best to show as many family groups as possible. The first Picture Book was intended to be a fair representation of all those families who lived at Llanteg during the latter part of the 19th and first half of the 20th century. This volume is intended to continue that theme, with more pictures of familiar old Llanteg faces. Many people have been included in both books but we believe that their different pictures will nonetheless be of interest to those who have fond memories of Llanteg in days gone by.

I feel it is a great privilege to have been able to collect all these wonderful old photographs of residents both past and present, and hope that these Picture Books will help to keep alive the memory of all these Llanteg people in years to come.

Again we have not acknowledged each photograph individually but would like to thank all those who have given us access to their family photographs over the years including:-

Winifred Baraclough, Lenna Beaven, Betty Bevan, Ruth Bevan, Tony Brinsden, Val Burke, Elwyn Callen, Margaret Carter, Alun Davies, Bob Davies, Denzil Davies, Eirian Davies, Eirwen Davies, John Davies, Kathleen Davies, Morfydd Davies, Ruth Davies, Eileen Deverell, Dennis Dudley, Bernard Dunbar, Maureen Ebsworth, Noel Ebsworth, Delmi Evans, Mary Evans, Jean Gardner, Ken George, Doreen Glanville, Ronnie and Audrey Glanville, Elizabeth Hall, Ken Hamilton, the late Margaret Hooper, Alwyn James, Audrey James, Betty James, the late Glyn James, Hugh and Mollie James, the late May James, Susan James, Josephine Jenkins, Nancy John, Sylvia Johnson, Jane Lawrence, Olive Lawrence, the late Wyn Lawrence, Hilary Lestner, John Lewis-Tunster, Katherine Lloyd, Simon Marklew, Alan Mason, Violet Merriman, Graham Mortimer,

Eileen Oriel, Beryl Payne, Allen Phelps, Kathleen Phillips, David Purser, Susan Richards, Sylvia Rogers, Connie Scourfield, Kay Scourfield, Marjorie Thomas, Avrenah Tremlett, Winifred Tunster, Owen Vaughan, George Vincent, Graham Ward, Olive Williams, Ray Wilson and the late Des Wolff.

Also a very big thank you to anyone whom we may have missed out; especially to Ray Wilson who gave us such well-captioned photographs for the first picture book and whom I inadvertently omitted from the list of contributors: your support is still very much appreciated.

We have tried to identify as many people as possible, but as some pictures go back virtually beyond living memory we apologise in advance for any omissions or mistakes.

I would also like to thank new member Ruth Webb who has helped me with proof reading, and Judith Lloyd who, despite leaving the area, still continues to be our trusty Editor.

Ruth Roberts

ERRATA
Llanteg - A Century in Photographs
Page 31 the photograph of the lady and baby should have been labelled 'Emily James with her niece Lucy Mathias'.
Page 90 should have stated that Annie and John Mathias of Pendeilo had *five* children - William, Pattie who died in her twenties, Albie who died young after being kicked by a horse, and twins Lucy and George.

FOREWORD

I was born at Blackheath in the parish of Crunwere on the 28th of April 1917. Many people call me Hugh Blackheath.

My parents, Howard and Emily James, were both born in Crunwere and lived there all their lives.

My father was the eldest son of Alfred and Elizabeth James of Broomy Lake. Alfred was a builder, well known locally and in the surrounding parishes. One can see evidence of his work in many places, from walls and stiles to barns and houses. Howard became a builder like his father and grandfather before him, and in my turn I also took up building as did my son after me - five generations of builders.

My mother was the daughter of William and Mary Davies of Blackheath. She was the youngest of their family of three boys and eight girls, several of whom married and settled in Crunwere or nearby parishes. We were related to many of the families living around and connected to others in various ways.

The Second World War brought changes which affected everyone. When war was declared I joined the army, and spent the next six and a half years serving my country. Some three to four of those years were spent abroad in India and Burma; a place far removed and very different from Llanteg.

The war over, it was time to come home and start living a normal life. I took up my old trade and started work as a builder once more. In the early fifties I married and built a home for my wife and family. It was the first private house to be built in the area for many years. We will have been living at Arfryn, near to Blackheath (next to Mountain Chapel), for fifty years in December. Here we brought up our children, and here our grandchildren come to see us and learn about their family history.

These books on the History of Llanteg in the parish of Crunwere are, in a way, telling a part of my life story. They tell of the way life was and the folk who lived here. This photograph book is full of familiar faces. Changes there have been, and always will be, but it is good to have a record to hand on to those who follow. The things that happen today are history tomorrow. I hope those who are responsible for these books will continue with the project until the record is up to date.

W. Hugh James

CONTENTS

CRUNWERE SCHOOL, 1909
We have been unable to identify these children but on the

following page is a list of everyone on the register at the time, with their year of birth in brackets.

CRUNWERE SCHOOL PUPILS IN 1909
As taken from the Admissions Book

ALLEN - William (Milton Back, 1899), Charles (Milton Back, 1900), Eleanor Mary (Milton Back 1902).

DAVIES - Wilfred George (The Griggs, 1900), William Henry (Sparrows Nest, 1901), Victor W.J.(The Griggs, 1901), Mabel (Sparrows Nest, 1903), Doris Irene (Milton, 1903).

GEORGE - Gwilym (The Downs, 1895), Elizabeth J. (The Downs, 1898), Arthur (The Downs, 1903).

GLANVILLE - Reginald Harcourt (Llanteague, 1897), Winifred Irene (Llanteague, 1898).

HODGE - Olwen Myfanwy (Mountain Farm, 1899), Mary (Mountain Farm, 1901), Thomas John (Mountain Farm, 1903).

HOWELLS -Thomas (Woodreef, 1895), Florence (Woodreef, 1900), Evelyn Jane (Woodreef, 1902).

JAMES - Herbert (Broomylake, 1894), William (Broomylake, 1896), David George (Castle Ely, 1897), Gladys May (The Cabin, 1897), Bertie (The Cabin, 1899), Margaret Elizabeth (The Cabin, 1903).

JONES - Amelia Ann (Castle Ely, 1895), Geoffrey Glanville (Heatherland, 1899), Noel (Heatherland, 1900).

LEWIS - Rowena (Oaklands, 1900).

MATHIAS - Martha Ann (Lower Pendeilo, 1900), William Edward (Lower Pendeilo, 1902), Albert John (Lower Pendeilo, 1903).

MORRIS - Annie (Furzy Park, 1895), Elizabeth (Furzy Park, 1897), Margaret (Furzy Park, 1900), Catherine (Furzy Park, 1902).

MORTIMER - John Steven (Summerbrook, 1896), May (Summerbrook, 1895), Amy (Summerbrook, 1899), Hannah Isabel (Summerbrook, 1904).

PHILLIPS - Gladys Mary (Middleton, 1895), Alice (Craftie, 1895), Mary Elizabeth (The Corner, 1896), Cissy (Craftie, 1898), Thomas Davies (Middleton, 1899), William Cyril (Craftie, 1899), Margaret Francis (Craftie, 1900), Mildred (Middleton, 1900), Florence May (Middleton, 1902), Ivor John (Craftie, 1902), William Leslie (Middleton, 1903).

REYNOLDS - Gwendoline (Belle Vue, 1897), Martha (Belle Vue, 1901).

SCOURFIELD - Cissie Maud (The Moors, 1896).

Crunwere School.

THE ALLEN FAMILY of ROSE COTTAGE and OXFORD

Rose Cottage.

John Allen and Janet Elizabeth with baby,
possibly Nellie.

John and Janet Elizabeth Allen with son John Henry (Jack).
The couple married in 1896 and lived at Rose Cottage.
John was the village blacksmith.

Willie Allen, the village postman, outside Blackheath.

Charlie Allen (father of Connie). Brother to Jack and Willie Allen of Rose Cottage. He later lived at Oxford.

Connie with husband Trevor Scourfield and son Desmond.

Connie (daughter of Charles and May Allen)
with husband Trevor Scourfield
and their children Maureen, Desmond and Janet.
Picture taken outside Oxford.

THE CALLEN FAMILY
Mary Callen
and
baby Elwyn.

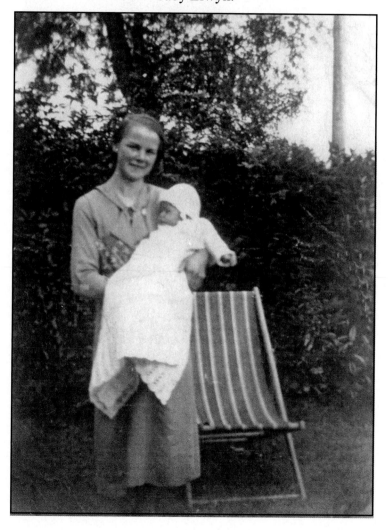

Wilfred and May Callen.

Back left - Elwyn Callen.

Elwyn Callen, 17 years old, 1955.
With Council Houses and School House in background.

THE DAVIES and JAMES FAMILIES of BLACKHEATH

Blackheath with Howard James.
Before the well-known porch was added.

Annie Thomas of Haverfordwest -
mother of Mary (born 1846/7) and mother-in-law to
William Davies of Blackheath.

Two sisters - Emily James (née Davies) and
Alice Philipps (née Davies) - daughters of
William and Mary Davies.

Emily James (née Davies)
with sons Hugh and Verdi.

Verdi, Herbert and Hugh James.
Sons of Howard and Emily James (née Davies).

Jack Davies, brother of Emily, who later lived at Kidwelly.

L. to r. George Mathias, Howard James, Howard's son Hugh, Howard's wife Emily, with their sons, Verdi with young Herbert on lap. About 1927/8.

Building Hillside, Tavernspite in 1933.
L. to r. Howard James, Charlie Allen, Willie James, Hugh James and Leslie Phillips.

Verdi James.

Note 'Library' sign on tree. Probably taken at Crunwere School.

Hugh James outside Blackheath, 1938.

Herbert James on bike.

Bertie James (brother to Howard), wife Mary, relative Ada Lowrie, Emily and Howard James. Outside the Five Arches in Tenby.

Herbert James, cousin Leslie Phillips (Middleton) and father Howard James.

Three sisters. Martha Mears (née Davies), Emily James (née Davies) and Lucy Jones (née Davies). Daughters of William and Mary Davies.

Cliff Williams and Hugh James (aged about 15 years).
Taken between Penparc and Carvan Chapel,
near Roger's Well, Tavernspite.

Herbert
James with
son Alan.
At Porthcawl
in the 1950s.

Alan James,
son of
Herbert and
Betty James,
with relative
George
Mathias -
on their way
to Caldey.

Howard James, grandson Ross and son Hugh.
Laying the foundation stones of Arfryn bungalow in mid 1950s.

Ross, Lewis and Janice, around 1960.
Children of Hugh and Mollie James.

THE DAVIES FAMILY OF BRYNELI
Noel Davies of Bryneli Farm.
Taken in 1952 at his degree ceremony
in Swansea University.

Willie and Alice Davies of Bryneli
with their son Noel.
At Swansea University degree ceremony, 1952.

THE DAVIES FAMILY of GREENACRE and STANWELL

Davies family group.

L. to r. back - William Davies, Robert Davies, John Davies (Johnny The Norton), Jim Davies.
L. to r. front - Lizzie Furzy Park, John Davies Greenacre, Cassie Three Wells.

Robert Davies, Greenacre, who emigrated in the 1890s.
Shown with his wife Stella and son Paul
on the beach in Santa Cruz, California, July 1908.
Robert was the son of John and Ann (née Richards).

John Davies Greenacre, died in 1928 aged 96 years.
Mr Davies had been born in Crunwere parish in 1832.

L. Bert Brinsden (husband of Alice Davies of Greenacre), during Second World War.

Bert Brinsden with mother-in-law Ann Davies 'Muz'.

Bob Davies Greenacre on marriage to Nora in 1946.

Bob and Nora Davies
outside No. 1 Council Houses, Llanteg.

Back left - Alice Brinsden standing behind
her mother Ann Davies outside Stanwell.
With them are Mr and Mrs Guirtoski
of Pendeilo Farm.

Arthur Davies
around 1950.
Uncle on visit from America.

THE DAVIES FAMILY of SPARROWS NEST

Sparrows Nest.

'Jim Sparrow', working in Colby Lodge Gardens, 1908-12. Jim had been born at Bevlin and married Margretta in 1901. She was the daughter of John James, the roadman, who lived at Rue[]wall.

Margretta 'Ret' Davies (née James) 1932 with her grandson.

Jim and Margretta Davies.

Amroth beach.
Margretta, her daughters Eleanor and Mabel,
sister-in-law Catherine (wife of Bill) and Catherine's son Jim.

Wilfred and Phoebe
Davies
(née Rees)
at Sparrows Nest.

Denzil Davies.

THE DAVIES FAMILY of TRENEWYDD
Betty, Iris, David and baby Olive,
children of William and Margaret Davies.
About 1930.

Eirwen Davies, later Mrs David Davies.

Dorothea Lawrence and Olive Davies on 'Kitty'.

Olive Davies aged about 17 years.

L. to r. Rev'd Bowen Harries
with Mr William Davies of Trenewydd.

L. to r. Iris Bowen (née Davies), father William Davies,
mother Margaret Davies and brother Ivor.

Garfield and Iris Bowen
(née Davies).

Betty Davies and Mary Bowen
(sister of Garfield Bowen).

Eirwen Davies with baby daughter Margaret.

David Vale of The Folly with young Alan
(son of Eirwen and David Davies) and Jake the dog.

Kathleen,
daughter of
Eirwen and David Davies.

THE GEORGE FAMILY of THE DOWNS

The Downs, around 1950.

Virginia George,
daughter of Richard.

L. Arthur George
ready to collect water from the Rectory Hill well.

Virginia 'Gini'
and her brother
Gwilym George

Centre front -
Gwilym George.

Ken George,
son of Arthur
and grandson
of Richard.

Ken George.

THE GLANVILLE FAMILY of EAST and WEST LLANTEG FARMS

East Llanteg Farm

West Llanteg Farm taken from Llanteg crossroads,
possibly 1930s.
Note the old metal railings that were there for many years.

At Wiseman's Bridge.
L. to r. Pattie Davies (Sparrows Nest),
Maggie Bowen (The Laurels),
Kathleen Williams 'Kess', and Hannah Glanville.

Tommy Glanville
at Llanteglos poultry farm
1938.

Margaret Glanville (later Mrs Hooper of Tenby).

Kathleen Morse (right) - first cousin to
Margaret and Hugh Glanville of East Llanteg Farm.

Wedding of Ronnie Glanville (West Llanteg) and Audrey Williams (Hillside, Tavernspite).

5th July 1947.

Betty Davies, Margaret Glanville and Donna Mortimer outside Mountain Chapel. With chimney just visible.

THE JAMES FAMILY of BEVLIN
Bertie James, Amroth Mill, during First World War.
Bertie was a brother to Frank James of Bevlin.

Connie James,
daughter of
Frank and Annie.
Died aged nine years
of diabetes, in 1931.

Betty James,
daughter of
Frank and Annie.

Geoffrey James,
son of
Frank and Annie.

Glyn James,
son of
Frank and Annie.

Audrey Rowlands,
Amroth 1946
(later to be Mrs Geoffrey James).

Alwyn James,
son of Betty and grandson of Frank and Annie,
outside Oaklands.

Maud Rowlands, aged about 16 or 17 years (later to become Mrs Glyn James).

Audrey James (née Rowlands) with her mother-in-law Annie James of Bevlin.

Roy James outside Oaklands in 1950s.

William Henry James, Bevlin, 1950s.

Three cousins - Robert James, Myfanwy Lloyd and Royston James, 1957.

Roy and Wendy James, 1957. Children of Geoffrey and Audrey James.

THE JAMES FAMILY of BROOMYLAKE

Broomylake.

Alfred James outside Broomylake.

Evelyn 'Lyn' Ebsworth (née James).
Lyn was born in 1891 and was the daughter of Alfred and
Elizabeth James (née Phillips).
She married William who was born in 1890.

In the garden. Alfred, son Bertie, Bertie's wife Mary and Alfred's wife Elizabeth.

Bertie James with his parents Elizabeth and Alfred. Elizabeth was the daughter of John and Elizabeth Phillips, The Corner. Alfred was born 1859, the son of William and Jane James of Broomylake, and married Elizabeth in 1888.

Alfred James with horses.

Mary with in-laws Elizabeth and Alfred James.

Outside Broomylake.
Maggie?, Alfred, Bertie and Mary.

Family group at beach.

Back - Willie Allen, Trevor and Connie Scourfield, Bertie James.
Front - three children of Trevor and Connie: Desmond, Maureen and Janet.

Three siblings - Lewis James (worked in Cardiff), Sarah (wife of George Davies, Parsonage Farm) and Alfred James (of Broomylake). Taken outside Elidyr Cottage.

THE LAWRENCE FAMILY

Two pairs of sisters

L. Sally Williams (later to be Mrs Lawrence, mother of Wyn and Rhys) with her sister - Mary Esther Murray (née Williams), second from right, who later went to Australia.

Second from left - Martha Jane Williams (née Phelps) with (r.) her sister Lilian James (née Phelps).

On horse - Morwen Lawrence.
L. to r. Nora, Eira, Rhys and Wyn Lawrence.
Taken at Trelessy.

Again on horse - Rhys and Dorothea Lawrence.

Ivor Davies (Amroth Farm), Wyn Lawrence (Trelessy), Bert Brinsden (Stanwell) and Mrs N.Davies (Elidyr Cottage).

Ivor Davies, Sarah Lawrence, Richard Evans Llanteglos
(kneeling), Ira Lawrence (kneeling), Robert Lawrence,
Dai Phillips (The Corner).

Land Army girls potato picking at Trelessy.

Wedding of Rhys Lawrence and Olive Davies of Trenewydd, 26th April 1952.

With Wyn and Dorothea Lawrence in background. The two small boys are John Bowen West Rose (son of Iris) and Keith Bevan Three Wells (son of Betty).

Wedding of Rhys Lawrence and Olive Davies of Trenewydd, 26th April 1952.
L. to r: Ivor Davies, Nora Davies (née Lawrence), William and Margaret Davies.
Back - Robert and Sally Lawrence.

Olive Lawrence with son Richard at Trelessy in 1956.

THE LEWIS FAMILY

Hughie Lewis (father of Winifred Tunster) with his two sons, Michael and with Ralph (on horse) - taken in 1940s at Gorse Hill, Pendine.

Winifred Tunster (née Lewis), aged 12 years.

THE MASON/ALLEN/JAMES FAMILY of RUELWALL

Mrs Sarah James
(née Lewis, Eileen Allen's maternal grandmother).

A few sheets of zinc were a luxury. Note the home-made shovel handle. Sarah had moved from the Rose Cottage area to Ruelwall when she married. She was the local midwife.

Emma James,
daughter of Sarah.

Sarah Jane Lloyd
(née James),
daughter of Sarah.
Picture taken at
Lampeter Velfrey.

Lizzie James
and baby.

Tom (son of Sarah) and wife Lizzie James,
Port Talbot.

Unknown female with Freddie and Ellen Allen
(Ellen was the eldest daughter of Sarah James).
Outside Ruelwall.

James Edgar John Mason,
later husband of Eileen Allen
(daughter of Freddie and
Ellen).

Alan Mason,
son of
John and Eileen Mason.

Barbara Mason,
daughter of
John and Eileen
Mason.

THE MORRIS FAMILY of FURZY PARK and THE LAURELS

Rebecca Raymond and Margaret (Maggie) Morris, later Bowen, outside The Laurels. Maggie was born in 1901 and the picture could have been in the 1920s.

Note the Victorian letterbox.

Elizabeth and Benjamin
Morris,
Furzy Park.

Benjamin Hancock
Morris
in wheelchair
with his brother
James.
Benjamin was father
to Ann
and grandfather
to Morfydd.

Dai Llantidwell
with Elizabeth Morris
and her daughter
Martha in front.

Richard H.Morris,
Furzy Park.

Ann Morris, Furzy Park.

David Anthony Richards.
Married Ann Morris

Bessie Morris, Furzy Park.

Martha Morris on right with friend.

L. to r. Bertie Bowen, Mr Allen the postman with Maggie Bowen (née Morris).
Outside The Laurels - telephone box on extreme right.

L. to r. unknown female with Maggie and Ivor Bowen outside The Laurels shop and Post Office.

Family wedding at Pilton Church.

L. to r. Sophie Morris, Ben Morris, Len Childs (groom), Amy Childs (née Morris, bride), Milly Davies and Reg Childs.

THE MORTIMER FAMILY of LEDGERLAND and SUMMERBROOK

Jack Mortimer,
Peter Phelps
and Harold Jones
(New House).

John
Steven
Mortimer
(Jack) on
the right
boxing
with
Berkley
John of
Kilgetty.

Ayah and Jack Mortimer at Ledgerland
with children
John Graham Dalton and Donna Christine.

Ayah Mortimer (née Phillips) outside Summerbrook.

Graham Mortimer and Rhys Lawrence shearing sheep at Summerbrook, 1959 or '60.

THE ORIEL FAMILY of GARNESS
The original Garness Farm.

Family group.
L. to r. Mary Oriel, daughter Maggie, husband Tom, daughter Ada, George Rosser (Mattie's husband) and in front young Geoffrey Rosser (Mattie's son).

Oriel family group - July 1954.

Freddie Oriel - last of the family to farm Garness.

THE PARSELL FAMILY of THE VALLEY

The Valley, 1955.

Gertrude Parsell.
Grandmother of Jean Gardner.

Baby Enid
with parents
Gert and George
Parsell,
about 1921/22.

Enid Parsell,
later Howells,
daughter of
George and Gert Parsell.

Gert and George Parsell
with daughter Enid
and Rose the dog,
about 1940,
at The Valley.

3rd August 1940
Wedding of
Andrew Evan Howells and Enid Parsell.

L. to r. friend of family - Walter?,
Andrew Evan Howells, Enid Parsell,
Betty John (cousin of Enid)
and Islwyn (relative of Andrew).

Andrew and Enid
Howells (née Parsell)
with daughter Jean
in 1942.

Enid Howells and Jean, 1945.

THE PHELPS FAMILY of SCHOOL HOUSE
(now SEABREEZE)

School House (now Seabreeze).

Garfield and Eleanor Mary 'Nellie' Phelps (née Allen of Rose Cottage).

Garfield and son Allen Phelps.

Betty
Shepherd
and
Nellie Phelps.

Olive Davies with Doreen Phelps
(sister of Allen and daughter of Garfield and Nellie).

Doreen Phelps with Herbert and Betty James
(née Shepherd).

THE PHILIPPS FAMILY of LLANTEGLOS

The Philipps family at Llanteglos around 1910.

The Philipps family at Llanteglos around 1910.

Llanteglos gardens
around 1910.

THE PHILLIPS FAMILY of CRAFTY (now CROFTY NURSERY)
Great aunt of Sarah Phillips, name unknown.

Sarah Jane Phillips 'Sally', born 1886.
Daughter of Joseph and Elizabeth (née Griffiths).
Married Jack Scourfield.

Thomas Daniel Phillips,
born 1891.
Son of Joseph and Elizabeth (née Griffiths).

Jack and Sarah Jane
Scourfield
(née Phillips).

Terry Phillips
with his cousin
from Cardiff
(taken outside
Stanwell).

Terry Phillips, born 1928.

THE PHILLIPS FAMILY of THE FOLLY
Fanny Fenn with her employer Rev'd Jackett.
Fanny had been born at South Stack Lighthouse.

Nancy Ethel Fenn Phillips, born 1931.
Picture taken mid 1930s.
Daughter of Fanny (née Fenn) and Thomas Phillips.

Nancy Phillips.

THE PHILLIPS FAMILY of MIDDLETON and SANDY GROVE

Middleton Farm
around 1920
with
Tom and Kitty
Phillips.

Sandy Grove,
possibly
1940s.

Catherine Mary Phillips 'Kitty'
(née Davies of Blackheath, born 1869).
Wife of Tom Phillips with grandson Lawrence,
early 1920s.

Thomas Davies Phillips with his wife, Mary Jane
Lawrence, and children Joan and Lawrence, 1920s.
Tom was born in 1899, the son of Tom and Kitty Phillips.

Three daughters of Tom and Kitty Phillips -
Florence kneeling (born 1902), Gladys back right
(born 1895) and Millie (born 1900)
with their nephew Lawrence (born 1921).

Millie Phillips,
psychiatric nurse at
Barnwood House,
Gloucester,
in early 1920s.

Millie Phillips
with her fiancé
Stan
who died of
consumption
before
they could marry.

Dora Phillips (née Harry), wife of Lawrence,
standing in the middle of the road outside Middleton
with Blackheath in the background.
The A477 was much quieter in the 1950s.

Tom Wilkins during First World War, in which he won the
Military Medal. He later married Gladys Phillips
and they went to live at Sandy Grove.

Young Ruth (daughter of Dora and Lawrence Phillips) with great aunts
Florence and Millie Phillips, and her sister Daphne on left.
Waiting for a bus outside the lower field gate (opposite Middleton) in September 1958.

THE ROGERS/COLLINGWOOD FAMILY

York House.

Tom Rogers,
1947.

Sylvia Collingwood with her father William
at Crunwere Church
before her marriage to Tom Rogers.

Tom Rogers and Sylvia (née Collingwood), Crunwere Church 1952.

THE SCOURFIELD FAMILY
George and Susannah Scourfield
with their three daughters,
Lizzie, Gwladys and Harriet.

Hilda and Hugh, children of Gwladys and Alfie Harris.
Lived at The Griggs.

Jack Scourfield,
about 1924.

Harriet and husband Bill with children Susie and Mary.
They lived at Lampeter Velfrey. Bill was lost at sea.

Rachel (née Scourfield) with husband Tom Roberts.
They lived at Glendale Terrace, Whitland.

Scourfield family group.

Centre is Susannah Scourfield with her two daughters Gwladys and Cissie. Also seven of Cissie's daughters and two of Gwladys's children. Unidentified boy front right. Cissie married Morgan Williams and lived at Velfrey Road, Whitland. Gwladys married Alfie Harris and lived at The Griggs, Llanteg.

Hugh and Donna.

James Scourfield,
son of George and Susannnah of The Moors.
Died of meningitis on 4th May 1907 aged 20 years.
Buried at Mountain Chapel.

Wedding of Dorothy 'Dolly' and Hugh Scourfield, 3rd August 1940.

L to r: Ivor Scourfield, Trevor Thomas, Hugh Scourfield, Dorothy Evans, Jack Stone and Frieda Scourfield.

Standing - Betty Lloyd of Bevlin, with Dolly May
Scourfield (née Evans - daughter of Catherine Llewellyn
and Thomas Evans). Believed to have been taken on
4th March 1941, Dolly's twenty-first birthday.

THE WILLIAMS FAMILY of LONG LANE
Nathanial 'Nat' Williams
with his chickens.

Nat Williams
pumping water
in the front garden of Long Lane.

Nat and Hannah Williams (née Callen)
Long Lane with
Katie Thomas
and unknown female.

Ruth Williams as baby.

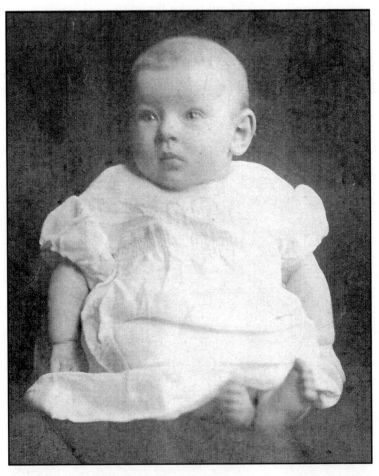

THE WILSON FAMILY of CASTLE ELY
Albert, Brynmor and Annie Wilson at
Castle Ely House, 1943.

THE WOLFF FAMILY of SCHOOL HOUSE
(now SEABREEZE)

Mr F.E.C.Wolff, headmaster of Crunwere School.
Taken in Croydon.

MISCELLANEOUS

Mr Wilkinson.
He was
the manager of
the poultry farm
at Llanteglos
and lodged at
Ruelwall.

Nurse Cousins,
the local
District Nurse.

Wedding of Myfanwy Herbert who had been an infants teacher at Crunwere School. She married a soldier and died young, aged 37 years.